LIKE A LADY

LIKE A LADY

Understanding God's Design

GWENDOLYN HARMON

Learning Ladyhood Press

To Abigail and Ana:
What a delight it has been to watch you each embark on your own journey of "learning ladyhood!" Thank you for letting me walk alongside you for a while.

Contents

PART 1

What is a Lady, Anyway?

I

Who am I?

Who am I? It's one of the most basic questions we can ask, but it's also one of the most important. There are so many voices and opinions out in the world about who you are and how you should view yourself, figuring out your identity can seem confusing. But those voices out there in the world, and even those closer to home, can never replace the truth of God's Word.

You see, the best place to go to figure out who you really are is to the God who created you, who knows you *even better* than you know yourself. Psalm 139 always helps me remember just how well God knows me, and the amazing thing is, He knows each and every person just as well!

"O Lord, Thou hast searched me, and known me.

Thou knowest my downsitting and mine uprising, Thou understandest my thought afar off.

Thou compassest my path and my lying down, and art acquainted with all my ways.

For there is not a word in my tongue, but, lo, O Lord, Thou knowest it altogether.

Thou hast beset me behind and before, and laid Thine hand upon me.

Such knowledge is too wonderful for me; it is high, I cannot attain unto it.

Whither shall I go from Thy Spirit? or whither shall I flee from Thy presence?

If I ascend up into heaven, Thou art there: if I make my bed in hell, behold, Thou art there.

If I take the wings of the morning, and dwell in the uttermost parts of the sea;

Even there shall Thy hand lead me, and Thy right hand shall hold me.

If I say, Surely the darkness shall cover me; even the night shall be light about me.

Yea, the darkness hideth not from Thee; but the night shineth as the day: the darkness and the light are both alike to Thee.

For Thou hast possessed my reins: Thou hast covered me in my mother's womb.

I will praise Thee; for I am fearfully and wonderfully made: marvellous are Thy works; and that my soul knoweth right well.

My substance was not hid from Thee, when I was made in secret, and curiously wrought in the lowest parts of the earth.

Thine eyes did see my substance, being yet unperfect; and in Thy book all my members were written, which in continuance were fashioned, when as yet there was none of them." (1-16)

Now, if you're at all like me, you probably just skipped over those verses to read what comes next. But they're worth another look. This time, take a pencil and mark all the things this passage says God knows. Think about them in terms of yourself, your life, the places you go, the thoughts you think, the words you speak. God knows all about all of it! And despite knowing everything, good *and* bad, He still loves us each individually.

Romans 8:38-39 tells us,

"For I am persuaded, that neither death, nor life, nor angels, nor principalities, nor powers, nor things present, nor things to come, Nor height, nor depth, nor any other creature, shall be able to separate us from the love of God, which is in Christ Jesus our Lord."

Of all the many voices telling you who you should be, or what you should be like, listen to the One who knows you best and loves you most: listen to your Creator.

2

Who Does God Say I Am?

Who does the Creator say you are? The best place to start is at the beginning. So, I want you to put down this book, go get your Bible, and read Genesis 1. Notice God's power and the purposeful way in which He created different things on the different days.

Did you read it? Ok. Now I want to point out one particular verse.

"So God created man in His own image, in the image of God created He him; male and female created He them." (v.27)

This verse is important for several reasons. First, it shows that gender was *God's* creation, not man's. It is in place right at the very beginning, in the first moments of human history. Gender cannot be a mere "social construct," because it existed before any kind of society.

This verse also shows us that gender existed before sin had entered into the world. This means that gender was not only created and defined by God, but also that it is *good*. In fact, after creating the first humans, God said what He had made was *very good*!

Because gender was God's idea, you can rest in the truth that your gender is not an accident or a coincidence, but a purposeful gift from God. You can trust that you are biologically exactly who God intended you to be!

Those who believe that gender is something you can choose to change miss the truth of a loving Creator who is both wise and purposeful in His determination of each person's gender.

The denial that gender is decided by God is not only a rejection of truth, but also the taking on of a responsibility we were never intended to bear. It puts upon each individual the enormous pressure of getting gender right. This is one reason why there is such depression and despair among those who reject God-given gender.

Without the absolute fact of biology to prove gender, how is anyone to know who they "really" are? Whenever the foundation of God's truth is removed, there can never be true certainty about anything.

Those promoting gender philosophies that reject God as the ultimate decider of gender promise freedom and happiness in becoming whoever you want to be. But instead, they lure people into a life of fear, uncertainty, and confusion.

You and I are not all-knowing like God, nor are we wise and perfectly good like He is. We are not equipped for the responsibility of deciding who or what we should be, because our Creator never intended us to make that decision. Instead, He made each of us purposefully, exactly how He wanted us to be, not only for His glory, but also for our good.

At some point in your life, you will probably be pressured to reject the gift of gender God has given you. When that pressure comes, you can stand firm on the truth that God created you on purpose, and He never makes mistakes.

Consider what God told the prophet Jeremiah:

> *"Before I formed thee in the belly I knew thee; and before thou camest forth out of the womb I sanctified thee, and I ordained thee a prophet unto the nations." (1:5)*

Before God formed you in your mother's womb, He knew you. Not only did He know all about you, He already had a plan for your life, and designed you with that plan in mind. Truly, you and I can say with the psalmist, *"I am fearfully and wonderfully made." (Psalm 139:14)*

3

What Does That Mean?

Now that we have looked at gender as a gift from God, let's look at what it means to be a woman according to the Bible. Since God designed gender, it makes sense that He would also define it, and our first clue is found in Genesis 2, which describes how woman came to be:

> "And the Lord God took the man, and put him into the garden of Eden to dress it and to keep it. And the Lord God commanded the man, saying, Of every tree of the garden thou mayest freely eat: But of the tree of the knowledge of good and evil, thou shalt not eat of it: for in the day that thou eatest thereof thou shalt surely die. And the Lord God said, It is not good that the man

should be alone; I will make him an help meet for him. And out
of the ground the Lord God formed every beast of the field, and
every fowl of the air; and brought them unto Adam to see what
he would call them: and whatsoever Adam called every living
creature, that was the name thereof. And Adam gave names to
all cattle, and to the fowl of the air, and to every beast of the
field; but for Adam there was not found an help meet for him."
(vv.15-20)

As Adam named the animals, there was not found *"an help
meet for him."* This phrase means "suitable helper" and highlights the earliest principle of Biblical ladyhood: you and I are
created to *help.* We were designed to find fulfillment in being
a helper.

Let's stop right there for a moment and apply this right
where we live. How are you a helper in your home? Do your
parents know they can count on you to help them when they
need you to? Do you come right away when they call your
name, or are you too absorbed in your own interests?

If you want to learn to be a godly lady, start by learning to
be a cheerful, observant, hard-working helper in your home.
And then learn to be that at church, school, or wherever else
you go! You'll be amazed at the joy and fulfillment God gives
when we simply live out our design.

Now, there's another aspect to ladyhood as a Genesis 2 helper. It is highlighted in the next verses:

> *"And the Lord God caused a deep sleep to fall upon Adam, and he slept; and he took one of his ribs, and closed up the flesh instead thereof; And the rib, which the Lord God had taken from man, made He a woman, and brought her unto the man. And Adam said, This is now bone of my bones, and flesh of my flesh: she shall be called Woman, because she was taken out of Man. Therefore shall a man leave his father and his mother, and shall cleave unto his wife: and they shall be one flesh." (v.21-24)*

Notice that this first woman was taken from man, brought by God to the man, and was to be made one with the man in marriage. Her purpose was linked with her relationship.

It is not that *all* women are meant to be helpers of *all* men. We are simply designed to fulfill our purpose within family life.

But contrary to the world's common accusation, woman was not intended to be a robot-like servant, or made an inferior creature to be bossed around. Rather, as Matthew Henry put it, "the woman was made of a rib out of the side of Adam; not made out of his head to rule over him, nor out of his feet to be trampled upon by him, but out of his side to be equal with him, under his arm to be protected, and near his heart to be loved."*

God designed men and women to fulfill different roles. Our culture pushes the idea that to be equal is to be interchangeable, but that is not the Biblical way of things.

God the Father, God the Son, and God the Holy Spirit have perfect unity and are equally God; yet, though the three make up just one God, the three Persons of the Trinity are distinct. They are different, but still equal. Biblical gender equality embraces the God-designed differences between male and female, without claiming one is inherently "better" than another.

Mankind as a whole is made in the image of God: created individually different, but equal. All are of equal value, but no individual is completely like another. Likewise, men and women are equally precious to God, though designed to be different and to fulfill different roles. Difference does not equal deficiency in the sight of God.

Of course, the role of woman as helper does not excuse or encourage man to be cruel, abusive or unloving. Rather, he is called to be a Christlike leader, accountable to God for how he treats the helper he has been given. Notice the command given to husbands in Ephesians 5:25-28.

> "Husbands, love your wives, even as Christ also loved the church, and gave Himself for it; That He might sanctify and cleanse it with the washing of water by the word, That He might present it to Himself a glorious church, not having spot, or wrinkle, or any such thing; but that it should be holy and without blemish. So ought men to love their wives as their own bodies. He that loveth his wife loveth himself."

Old and New Testament agree that men are to be the leaders in the home, church, and society. Yet, with the authority of leadership comes a responsibility to lead well.—A responsibility for which each man will personally answer to God.

The world likes to point to examples of women who have been mistreated by a male authority as reasons to reject Biblical gender roles, yet mankind's sin does not negate the goodness of God's design. Don't let the cynicism of our society destroy your view of God's design for men and women.

Leaders will not always lead well, but throughout the Bible God gives us examples of how God used a willing helper to have an amazing impact, even though they served under an ungodly authority.

As women, we will each answer to God for how we fulfill our role as helper, regardless of how our leaders lead. As we close out this chapter, think about the authorities in your life. How does God want you to be a help?

*Matthew Henry's Commentary Zondervan: Grand Rapids. 1960 p.7

4

Eve, the Serpent, and
Some Fig Leaves

Genesis 1-2 tells us how and why woman was made and gives us a foundational concept of what God has designed us to do. Genesis 3 adds to that concept and also shows us why it is often so difficult for women to accept their Biblical role.

Genesis 3 begins with the introduction of a new character into the Biblical narrative. Up to this point, we have seen God at work creating everything that exists, and giving special attention and instruction to the first man and woman. But now a serpent appears on the scene.

> *"Now the serpent was more subtil than any beast of the field which the Lord God had made. And he said unto the woman, Yea, hath God said, Ye shall not eat of every tree of the garden? And the woman said unto the serpent, We may eat of the fruit of the trees of the garden: But of the fruit of the tree that is in the midst of the garden, God hath said, Ye shall not eat of it, neither shall ye touch it, lest ye die." (vv.1-3)*

God's command not to eat of the tree of the knowledge of good and evil had been given to Adam as the leader, *(2:16-17)* he had apparently passed it along to Eve. But instead of trying to get Adam to disobey God, Satan went to *Eve* with his tempting lies.

Eve was the one under authority, but Satan pushed her to make her own independent decision. Adam wasn't even mentioned in the conversation. Eve knew what God had said about the fruit from that particular tree, and if she had taken the matter to Adam, his leadership would have strengthened her to resist temptation.

Not that Adam was immune to temptation (after all, he eventually ate the fruit, too,) but two are stronger than one and Adam had the certainty of having been given the command by God Himself.

Satan then moved from questioning to outright denial:

> *"And the serpent said unto the woman, Ye shall not surely die: For God doth know that in the day ye eat thereof, then your eyes shall be opened, and ye shall be as gods, knowing good and evil." (v.4-5)*

This combination of questioning and denial of God's truth is in fact exactly what we see in our world today in this area of Biblical womanhood. Perhaps you have even thought as you read this book, "Surely God couldn't have meant *that!*"

The idea of God designing man and woman to fulfill different gender-specific roles is not a popular one, and the idea that Eve *needed* her husband's leadership might strike you as wrong, but notice what we are told in 1 Timothy 2:14,

> *"And Adam was not deceived, but the woman being deceived was in the transgression."*

Adam sinned, to be sure, and as the leader, the entering of sin into the world is laid squarely upon his shoulders. Romans 5:12 tells us,

> *"Wherefore, as by one man sin entered into the world, and death by sin; and so death passed upon all men for that all have sinned"*

Yet though he did sin, he was not deceived. Eve, however, was.

Now, we have to be careful not to read more into this than the Bible states. The facts are: Satan definitely targeted Eve. She was definitely deceived by Satan's lies. Adam was definitely *not* deceived but chose to sin anyway, once Eve had.

This doesn't mean women are intellectually inferior or morally lacking (both sinned.) It simply illustrates the truth that God designed the husband to lead and the wife to respond.

An overview of the Bible will show that one of Satan's most common tricks is to get women to step out and take matters into their own hands. In our culture, that has now become the norm, but it was never God's design. Men may fail in their leadership, and women may feel they "have to" step up to fill the gap, but that is not how God designed things to work.

Back in Genesis 3, we see Satan targeting Eve when she was on her own. Eve fell for Satan's deception; and, instead of relaying this "new information" to Adam, she decided to take a look at the fruit.

> "And when the woman saw that the tree was good for food, and that it was pleasant to the eyes, and a tree to be desired to make one wise, she took of the fruit thereof, and did eat, and gave also unto her husband with her, and he did eat." (v.6)

Eve's focus was on what the fruit could do for *her*, rather than on what *God* had said was right. Satan often uses this kind of self-focus to distract us. When you hear the world arguing against the Biblical pattern of femininity, notice what they emphasize: how you feel, what you want, what makes you happy—these are not solid foundations upon which to build your life.

If you have asked Christ to be your Savior, He calls you to a life focused on serving Him (often by serving others.) A godly lady rejects the world's call to focus on herself, and chooses to live her life for God. His will, His word, and His desires for her life are her highest authority and her deepest delight.

But back to Eve. Sin always has consequences, as James 1:14-15 tells us:

> "But every man is tempted, when he is drawn away of his own lust, and enticed. Then when lust hath conceived, it bringeth forth sin: and sin, when it is finished, bringeth forth death."

God had told Adam that the day they ate the fruit, they would die. And that process of death *did* begin that day, physically, and in their position before God, as sinners destined for eternal spiritual death. But they did not see the results right away.

Perhaps Eve thought it was fine, because she didn't drop dead after one bite of the fruit, but one thing did change. She and Adam noticed something they had never thought to notice before:

> *"And the eyes of them both were opened, and they knew that they were naked; and they sewed fig leaves together, and made themselves aprons." (v.7)*

God made mankind perfect and without sin, but as soon as sin entered into the hearts of the first man and woman, their nakedness became a shame to them, and they tried to cover themselves up. This is the foundation of the principle of modesty, which occurs periodically throughout the Bible.

From this point on, nakedness is spoken of in the Bible as a shameful thing, not because of how God created us, but because of the sin in our hearts. Because of sin, we now need to be careful to cover our bodies. Here, too, the world tries to make us believe that the Bible's view of nakedness is wrong, that it's no big deal to show this or that part of the body, or to look at art that features unclothed figures. But the Bible is clear that *because of sin* the human body is to be covered.

And clothes weren't just Adam and Eve's idea. If you read on, you'll see in verse 21 that,

> "Unto Adam also and to his wife did the Lord God make coats of skins, and clothed them."

I'm sure those coats of skin covered more than Adam and Eve's hastily-constructed fig leaf aprons!

As you read through the Bible for yourself, notice what God calls nakedness, notice what He says about it, and ask God to show you how to dress in a way that pleases Him.

5

The Curse and God's Purpose

You may have heard people talk about "the curse." In Biblical circles, that refers to the consequences of Adam and Eve's sin on all mankind. After Adam and Eve sinned, God came to walk with them in the garden as He usually did. (Just imagine!)

But instead of coming to greet their Creator, Adam and Eve cowered in the foliage, hiding from Him in shame. God, of course, knew exactly where they were, but gave them the opportunity to come out of hiding on their own.

> *"And the Lord God called unto Adam, and said unto him, Where art thou?" (v.9)*

After Adam explains that he was ashamed to be seen because of his nakedness, God asks another convicting question:

> *"Who told thee that thou wast naked? Hast thou eaten of the tree, whereof I commanded thee that thou shouldest not eat?" (v.11)*

What happens next reminds me of a line of falling dominoes: Adam blames Eve, Eve blames the serpent, and no one takes responsibility for their actions. –How like you and me!

It is so easy to blame others for what we ourselves have chosen to do. God wasn't impressed by the blame game, however, and held each one responsible for their own part in the situation. This is what we refer to as "the curse." He starts with the serpent:

> *"And the Lord God said unto the serpent, Because thou hast done this, thou art cursed above all cattle, and above every beast of the field; upon thy belly shalt thou go, and dust shalt thou eat all the days of thy life: and I will put enmity between thee and the woman, and between thy seed and her seed; it shall bruise thy head, and thou shalt bruise his heel." (v.14-15)*

This is the first promise of Jesus, the "seed" of the woman who would bruise the head of the serpent. (The Hebrew word for *bruise* has the idea of snapping at or crushing.) There is much that could be said about this, but that isn't our focus in this study.

After declaring the certain defeat of the serpent, God talks to Eve:

> "Unto the woman He said, I will greatly multiply thy sorrow and thy conception; in sorrow thou shalt bring forth children; and thy desire shall be to thy husband, and he shall rule over thee." (v.16)

This one verse describes much of what it means to be a woman now that sin has entered into the world. It can basically be boiled down to two concepts:

SUBMISSION

Interestingly, the idea of man being the leader is present *before* Adam and Eve sinned, but one of the consequences of sin has to do with women's *attitude* towards that leadership. The woman's desire would be towards her husband, and he would rule over her.

Ever since Eve chose to disobey God, women have been bothered by the concept of man as the leader. Whether because they feel their male authority is "doing it wrong" or that they could do it better, women's natural (sinful) tendency is to push her way into the leadership position given to man. That is why 1 Timothy 2:12 reminds us that women are not to *"usurp authority over the man"* in the context of the church, but instead to *"learn in silence, with all subjection." (2:11)*

Some will argue that Paul hated women, or that the New Testament writers were just expressing their own personal opinions in the numerous New Testament passages on the role of women in the church and home, but that is simply not the case.

This authority structure within the church (as well as that within the home) is based on the order of God's creation, and reinforced by God's declaration to Eve in Genesis 3:16. Besides that, those passages are included in the Bible *because* they were inspired by the Holy Spirit. God Himself put them in His Word and set His stamp of approval on them as His truth.

The Biblical authority structure in the home and in the church is for man to lead (himself following Christ's leading) and for women to be in submission to that leadership. What this means is that women are to be just what God created us to be: helpers who follow and support the leadership of their God-given male authority, (primarily a husband or father.)

Within the church, this means that we are to have humble hearts that are ready to listen, learn, and be helpers for the cause of Christ and the health of our local church.

What it does not mean is for every woman to be in subjection to every man. Notice that Eve's desire would be to *her* husband, and *he* would rule over her. It also does not mean that man has the God-given right to rule over women however they please. After all, Adam had his own part in God's Genesis 3 "curse."

> "And unto Adam He said, Because thou hast hearkened unto the voice of thy wife, and hast eaten of the tree, of which I commanded thee, saying, Thou shalt not eat of it: cursed is the ground for thy sake; in sorrow shalt thou eat of it all the days of thy life; Thorns also and thistles shall it bring forth to thee; and thou shalt eat the herb of the field; In the sweat of thy face shalt thou eat bread, till thou return unto the ground; for out of it wast thou taken: for dust thou art, and unto dust shalt thou return."(vv. 17-19)

Notice that God includes Adam's failure to lead his wife as part of his sinful disobedience. God holds men to high standards of leadership, and the failure of men to lead well does not excuse women from responding in a Biblical way to their leadership. (See 1 Peter 3 for more about this.)

Before we move on to the next aspect of what it means to be a woman, remember that the principle of male leadership was in place *before* sin. God's proclamation of judgment in Genesis 3:16 had more to do with women's attitude towards his leadership than the fact of his leadership itself. As Matthew Henry says,

> "The sentence was not a curse, to bring her to ruin, but a chastisement, to bring her to repentance."*

Eve's decision to sidestep her husband's authority (and with it, his protection) was inseparably linked to her decision to disobey God's command concerning the fruit. Both were acts of disobedience. Eve needed (and you and I still need) the reminder of God's design because with her new sin nature, her natural tendency would forever be to pridefully usurp Adam's role as leader.

LIFE-BEARING

The other foundational aspect of what it means to be a woman is found not just in Genesis 3:16, but also in Adam's response to God's declaration of judgment in 3:20. Immediately after the description of how things were going to be for men and women because of sin, we find this surprising statement:

> "And Adam called his wife's name Eve; because she was the mother of all living."

From the place of this verse within the narrative of the verses surrounding it, I get the impression that Adam heard God's words, then immediately gave his wife a name. This might seem odd to you—it does to me! But if you read back through Genesis up to this point, Eve is simply referred to as "the woman," or as Adam's wife. Now, the first woman gets a name—one that highlights a basic part of her role in life.

The name "Eve" literally means "life-bearer." As women, we are designed to be life-bearers. We are given bodies designed to nurture and sustain a new life from conception to birth, and to feed that new life until it is ready to eat "solid" food. Physically speaking, women are made for motherhood.

Our culture sneers at women who choose to make motherhood their life, but motherhood is a beautiful and precious part of being a woman. This isn't limited to the physical process of pregnancy and birth, either. We are designed to be life-bearers emotionally and spiritually as well, and this is where the concept of life-bearer becomes universal.

God may or may not have marriage and motherhood in His plan for your life, but spiritual "life-bearing" is His plan for all Christian women. Look at what Titus 2 says:

> "The aged women likewise, that they be in behaviour as becometh holiness, not false accusers, not given to much wine, teachers of good things; That they may teach the young women to be sober, to love their husbands, to love their children, to be discreet, chaste, keepers at home, good, obedient to their own husbands, that the word of God be not blasphemed." (vv.3-5)

We'll look at this passage again later on, but for now, notice the role of the "aged" women in the church: they are to teach the younger women. Though we have seen from 1 Timothy 2 that women are not to teach the church as leaders or authorities, God not only allows, but *intends* that Christian women teach each other. This is spiritual life-bearing in action.

As I write this little book, God has not chosen marriage or motherhood for me. But He has chosen to use me to "teach" other women what He is teaching me about being a woman as He defines womanhood. Though His plan has not included physical life-bearing, I nevertheless am expected to use His gift of my gender to nurture and teach other women.

But we must remember that God's plan for the older women to teach requires the younger women to learn. After all, we cannot teach that which we have not learned ourselves! Whatever phase of life you are in, be quicker to listen and learn than to jump in with what you have to share.

A Christian woman is to be both teacher and student, usually at the same time.

As a teen, I had the privilege of being taught by several key "older" ladies. The way in which each one invested in me was different, but the two things they all had in common were time and prayer. Time spent with a sister in Christ, bathed in prayer and reliance on the Holy Spirit can make a life-changing difference. It did for me.

What will spiritual life-bearing look like for you? It may mean helping in the nursery or a Sunday School class. It could mean spending time helping a young mother cook or clean or take the children on an outing. It could mean humbly coming alongside a peer to gently point out something in her life that does not line up with God's Word, or to encourage her by sharing how God is helping you grow in Him.

Spiritual life-bearing looks slightly different for each person, and it is important to let God be the one leading you as you seek to live out His life-bearing design for you.

*Matthew Henry's Commentary Zondervan: Grand Rapids. 1960 p.11

PART 2

Like a Lady: Inside and Out

Now that we've looked at the gift of gender, and who God says we are as women, let's focus for a while on character. As we have already seen, God's design for us as women extends far beyond the physical fact of being born female. That is the difference between becoming a woman and becoming a godly lady.

You see, all it takes to become a woman is to grow older, but to become a *lady* in the sense we are using it in this book requires a work of God in the heart to develop Christlike character. We are created to be helpers and life-bearers, but to fulfill those roles well on the outside, we must first learn to be "like a lady" on the inside.

6

Where Do I Begin?

So, where do we start on this journey into Biblical lady-hood? Well, the best place to start any journey is with the ground beneath your feet. Let's look at what God has to say to you in the season of girlhood:

"Children, obey your parents in the Lord: for this is right. Honour thy father and mother; (which is the first commandment with promise;) that it may be well with thee, and thou mayest live long on the earth." Ephesians 6:1-3

"Children, obey your parents in all things: for this is wellpleasing unto the Lord." Colossians 3:20

The first step to Christlike ladyhood is honor and obedience to your parents. At least, it was mine. I had grown up in a Christian home where I was taught to obey my parents, but as a teen, I let myself wallow in self-pity and allowed bitterness to sour my relationship with my parents. I was rebellious—at least internally—and behaved as if the verses above had never been included in the Bible.

If it hadn't been for God's merciful intervention, I would have destroyed my life in pursuit of being like "everyone else." Want to know what turned me around?

In a word, humiliation.

God had brought a teacher into my life who recognized the lack of obedience and honor to my parents, and God led her to give me a rather unusual assignment. Each time my parents told me no, I had to *thank them*.

The first time it happened, it took what seemed like an eternity to conquer my pride enough to squeak out a "thank you" before running off to my room. But it was what I needed.

Slowly, but surely, the Holy Spirit took that one act of humble obedience and led me step by step down a path of spiritual growth that not only deepened my relationship with God, but also my relationship with my parents.

God commands *both* obedience and honor; and, as someone once pointed out to me, there is no expiration date on this command. While the Bible teaches that marriage transfers you from your father's authority to your husband's, there is never an ending point for honoring your parents.

If you want to fulfill your role as a husband's helper, you need to learn the childhood lessons of honor and obedience. These will not only prepare you to accept and support your husband's leadership, it will also help you learn how to honor and obey God.

The journey from girlhood to ladyhood is simply a matter of growing in the Lord. As you obey Him each day, reading His Word and spending time talking to Him in prayer, the Holy Spirit will show you each next step along the way.

The goal of this study isn't to give you some magical formula or list to check off that will make you a godly lady. Instead, I hope this gives you a glimpse of where you're headed. To that end, let's take another look at Titus 2, this time to see what God wants you to be like on the inside.

7

Learning Ladyhood

"The aged women likewise, that they be in behaviour as becometh holiness, not false accusers, not given to much wine, teachers of good things; That they may teach the young women to be sober, to love their husbands, to love their children, to be discreet, chaste, keepers at home, good, obedient to their own husbands, that the word of God be not blasphemed." (vv.3-5)

Let's take a look at what you as a "young woman" are to be learning:

To be Sober

The definition of this word is "of sound mind," and can have the idea of being disciplined or corrected. It makes me think of times as a child when my friends and I were having a riotous good time playing, and a teacher or parent had to correct one of us. Maybe you can relate to the awkward silence and the subdued, cautious behavior that followed.

We still had fun, but there was a seriousness brought about by appropriate correction or discipline. That is what it means to be taught to be sober. A Titus 2 lady will not bluster through life heedlessly, but will be sober, sound-minded enough to exercise appropriate caution and seriousness.

To Love Husband and Children

You may be thinking that it seems odd for women to have to be taught a proper love for husband and children. I mean, doesn't that come automatically? Well, not exactly. There's the kind of love the world pushes, love that is all emotion; and then there is Christlike love, which is self-sacrificing and based not on feelings, not on what the loved one can do for me, but on what I can do for the good of the loved one. That kind of love does not come naturally, and all of us need reminders at times to love our family members as Christ loves them.

To be Discreet

This word literally means self-controlled, and has the idea of being sane or moderate. Self-control (also called temperance) is crucial to the Christian life, and is in fact one characteristic of the fruit of the Spirit (Galatians 5:23.) As ladies who have the Holy Spirit indwelling and empowering us, our self-control should be one of our defining qualities.

In my experience, self-control is often developed inch by inch, but lost mile by mile. Godly "aged women" can help us learn to develop self-control, and can also point out areas of our lives in which we are letting self have free reign.

To be Chaste

This word literally means "clean," though it is easy to see by the context that it is intended to mean more than just physical cleanliness. *Chaste* has the idea of innocence, modesty, or perfection. Contrary to our culture, which pushes us to be "hot" or "sexy," God wants us to develop innocence and purity of heart and life—and to reflect His purity on the inside *and* the outside.

It is easy for younger women to get caught up in fads or trends that don't line up with God's idea of purity, or to dive into media that does not feed a heart and mind of innocent purity.

Listen well to the godly "aged" women God brings into your life. They have experience and maturity and can be valuable protectors of your innocence and purity. Pay attention not just to their words, but also to their example. Why do they wear what they wear, say what they say, choose what they choose?

To be a Keeper at Home

This phrase means just what it says: someone who stays at home, who is domestically inclined. I had the joy of growing up with a "stay-at-home mom" and reaping the benefits of her choice to be a keeper at home. From her and other Titus 2 lady teachers, I learned to value the home, to see the keeping of a home as not a duty, but as a privilege.

To be Good

This one is pretty self-explanatory. Perhaps it is because I grew up in a generation that used the words "sick" and "wicked" as slang for anything they thought praiseworthy; but it has always been easy for me to see how goodness is a quality we do not naturally exhibit or value. God is good—perfectly good—and as Christians, we are to reflect His goodness. This can only be done through the power of the Holy Spirit, but He often uses godly people to help us learn to reflect His goodness. This is partly what Proverbs 27:17 speaks of:

> "Iron sharpeneth iron; so a man sharpeneth the countenance of his friend."

To be Obedient (to your own husband)

In part one of this book we looked at the Biblical design for family structure. You will remember that God holds men responsible for being good leaders, but even a godly husband is but a sinner saved by grace. This is partly why young women need to be taught to be obedient to their own husbands.

No wife is perfect, and no marriage is perfect, but I have learned much over the years by just observing godly "aged" women. Notice how they speak to and about their husbands, how they respond when they disagree, what they do to honor or encourage their husbands.

As you observe and learn from these godly older ladies, treasure up the good things you observe as an example, and (because they, too, are sinners saved by grace,) take any failures or negatives as a warning.

8

Respect, Meekness, and Trust

Another passage that deals with the character of a godly lady is 1 Peter 3. This has much to do with married life, but I am including it here because it demonstrates just how powerful godly ladyhood is when lived in surrender to the will of God.

It also highlights a few important qualities a godly lady should aim to develop.

> "Likewise, ye wives, be in subjection to your own husbands; that,
> if any obey not the word, they also may without the word be won
> by the conversation of the wives; While they behold your chaste
> conversation coupled with fear."(vv.1-2)

Let's stop here for a moment and look at these two verses.
We see here another command for women to be in subjection
(same word as *obedient* in Titus 2:5) to their own husbands, but
then it takes a different turn.

Notice the phrase *"if any obey not the word."* This literally
means to willfully disbelieve the Word of God. So, this passage
is giving instruction to Christian women with husbands who
aren't just not saved yet, but are willfully and intentionally not
believers.—Does that sound like an easy situation to you?

If ever there were a reason for an exception to the rule of
family authority structure, you would think this would be it.
But look at what God says will happen if the believing wives
simply keep on doing right in the eyes of God:

> "that, if any obey not the word, they also may without the word
> be won by the conversation of the wives"

Conversation here means behavior or manner of life. As these women behave with purity and fear, (yes, that's really the word fear, but it can be used to convey the idea of reverence as well,) God can use that to turn the heart of the stubbornly disbelieving husband to Himself.

Now, let's look at the next few verses, which give a fuller look at what this "chaste conversation" will look like:

> *"Whose adorning let it not be that outward adorning of plaiting the hair, and of wearing of gold, or of putting on of apparel; But let it be the hidden man of the heart, in that which is not corruptible, even the ornament of a meek and quiet spirit, which is in the sight of God of great price. For after this manner in the old time the holy women also, who trusted in God, adorned themselves, being in subjection unto their own husbands: Even as Sara obeyed Abraham, calling him lord: whose daughters ye are, as long as ye do well, and are not afraid with any amazement."* (vv.3-6)

In my early teens, I went through a phase where I always wore my hair in two braids. The first time I noticed this verse was at a Bible study where we were reading through the passage, taking turns each reading a verse. Guess which verse my turn fell on? I remember my face feeling hot as I read the part about plaited (braided) hair and joked afterwards, "I guess I picked the wrong hairstyle!"

Even then I knew enough to know that the verse wasn't talking about my two simple braids, but I wasn't sure exactly what it was talking about. Can you relate?

So, what is the point of the verse if it isn't telling us we can't braid our hair or wear gold or put on clothes? Think about the time period this was written in. From what I have read, the women of that time used elaborately braided hairstyles, gold jewelry, and flamboyantly expensive clothing as a status symbol—like some people use expensive designer purses or shoes today. The point here is that the focus should not be on how we look outside, but who we are inside.

When people look at you, what do they see? Are you known for your outside, or for your inside? The goal is for the two to match. We cannot avoid making choices about what we will wear or how we will do our hair, but a godly lady will have a heart that seeks to reflect the character of Christ in how she dresses.

To make this point clearer, look at what it says we *are* to adorn ourselves with:

"But let it be the hidden man of the heart, in that which is not corruptible, even the ornament of a meek and quiet spirit, which is in the sight of God of great price." (v.4)

You and I have the opportunity to adorn ourselves with something which *God* greatly values.

I have often heard this idea of a meek and quiet spirit dismissed over the years by women who think it simply isn't "who they are." But the Bible doesn't limit a meek and quiet spirit to those who are naturally shy or have quiet personalities. A meek and quiet spirit is something we can all adorn ourselves with, no matter what our personality.

The word for *meek* here means mild or humble. It reminds me of the description of charity, or Christlike love, in 1 Corinthians 13:4-7

> *"Charity suffereth long, and is kind; Charity envieth not; charity vaunteth not itself, is not puffed up, Doth not behave itself unseemly, seeketh not her own, is not easily provoked, thinketh no evil; Rejoiceth not in iniquity, but rejoiceth in the truth; Beareth all things, believeth all things, hopeth all things, endureth all things."*

The word for *quiet* in 1 Peter 3:4 comes from a root that means "keeping one's seat." It has the idea of stillness, tranquility, and peace. A meek and quiet spirit is able to face irritation, annoyance, or alarm with stillness and gentleness. This can only be done through the power of the Holy Spirit, which He gives us as we choose to act in obedience to Him.

The next two verses give an example that always surprises me:

> "For after this manner in the old time the holy women also, who trusted in God, adorned themselves, being in subjection unto their own husbands: Even as Sara obeyed Abraham, calling him lord: whose daughters ye are, as long as ye do well, and are not afraid with any amazement."

Compared to our modern society, the women of the Old Testament did often exhibit a striking level of submission and respect for their husbands. But *Sarah*?

If you read the chapters in Genesis that tell us about her life, you will notice her taking matters into her own hands on more than one occasion. However, another careful reading will reveal times when she *did* obey her husband.

Interestingly, the most obvious of those are both times when Sarah could have argued that her husband was leading her the wrong way; but she obeyed, and God commends her for it.

Notice what her example and that of the other "holy women" of the Old Testament times have in common. They are all women *"who trusted in God."*

Their trust in God motivated them to adorn themselves with a meek and quiet spirit, obeying God by submitting to their husbands, even when they didn't necessarily agree with how their husbands were leading them.

So what does all this have to do with you, now, in this season of life? Now is the time to develop the godly adorning of a meek and quiet spirit, to learn to behave with purity and reverence, and to submit to our authorities with a right attitude, whether or not we agree with them.

Some of you may be voicing the age-old objection, "But what if my authority tells me to do something wrong?" If you are asking that, you probably already know the answer. It is a question that is not usually asked from a heart that honestly wants to know. Most often, it is a question asked as a means of creating an excuse to disobey authorities.

But I'll answer the question just in case: Authorities are sinful human beings (as are you) so there is a possibility an authority will one day ask you to do something that goes against the clear commands of the Bible. However, if you have asked Christ to forgive your sins, accepting His gift of salvation, the Holy Spirit lives inside you. And one of the reasons He is there is to guide you.

No situation is too difficult or complicated or messy for the Holy Spirit to handle.

Take for your example Sarah and the women of the Old Testament, whose response to their authorities was determined by their trust in God. If you are walking close to God, seeking to obey Him and choosing to act out of trust rather than fear, anger, or rebellion, God will help you know what to do in each and every situation you face.

9

⚜

Putting it All Together

The process of learning to be a lady in a Biblical sense is just that: a process. It is a journey with many ups and downs, but my prayer for you as you embark upon the quest for godly ladyhood is that it will be a journey you make hand in hand with God.

On the following page are some ideas of things you can be praying for and about as you seek Him and His will for your life:

Lord, help me see myself as You see me.

Help me value my gender and my roles of helper and life-bearer as You value them.

Show me how to live out those roles in my life today.

Protect my heart from being deceived by Satan's lies.

Help me be on guard against charging into a role that is not mine to take.

Help me learn to be submitted to my authorities with a meek and quiet spirit, trusting You to take care of me.

Help me to be teachable now as You prepare me for what You have planned for my future.

About the Author

Gwendolyn Harmon is a teacher, writer, and church musician who loves to encourage Christian ladies to be all that God designed them to be. She is the author of the *Hymns for the Heart* devotional series and several devotional-level commentaries, in addition to Learning Ladyhood, a blog about the journey of becoming a godly lady. To learn more, visit **www.learningladyhood.com**.

Other Books by Learning Ladyhood Press

Devotional Commentaries:

- *Contentment: Truths from Proverbs 30:7-9*
- *Blessed: a Study of the Beatitudes*
- *Fruitful: a Study of the Fruit of the Spirit*
- *Think on These Things: a Study of Philippians 4:8*

Hymns for the Heart Devotional Series:

- *Tune My Heart*
- *Hark*
- *Risen*
- *Jesus, I Come*
- *We Gather Together*

Wholesome Fiction:

- *Katherine of Harborhaven: a New Beginning*